T0359557

CATCH FIRE: Friendly Street Poets 33

Aidan Coleman was born in Aberystwyth, Wales in 1976 and lived in Nottingham, Wollongong, the Barossa and Gawler before settling in Adelaide. He has been published in a number of journals and newspapers in Australia, the UK and the USA. His poems have appeared in a number of anthologies, including the *Best Australian Poems* of 2005 and 2006, and have been performed on ABC Radio National's *Poetica*. His first collection of poems, *Avenues & Runways*, published by Brandl & Schlesinger in 2005, was short-listed for the New South Wales Premier's Literary Award. He is also an English teacher and a passionate promoter of Shakespeare and poetry in schools for which he received an ASG Community Merit Medal.

Juliet A. Paine is a local South Australian, born in 1979 and raised in Adelaide, and has also spent three years living in Hobart. She attended Saint Peters' Girls' School in Stonyfell and the University of Adelaide graduating with a BA Honours (First Class) in English. Her poetry, articles and short fiction have appeared in both local and national journals and newspapers including *The Australian*, *Five Bells*, *Voiceworks*, and *Famous Reporter*. Her first collection of poems, *Poems for a Paranoid Generation*, was published by Ginninderra Press in 2001. She has also won numerous grants and academic awards. She is currently a senior English teacher at Loreto College, Marryatville.

CATCH FIRE

Friendly Street Poets 33

Edited by

Aidan Coleman and Juliet A. Paine

Friendly Street Poets in association with Wakefield Press

Friendly Street Poets Incorporated
PO Box 3697
Norwood
South Australia 5000
friendlystreetpoets.org.au

in association with

Wakefield Press
1 The Parade West
Kent Town
South Australia 5067
www.wakefieldpress.com.au

First published 2009

Copyright © of all poems remains the property of the authors
Copyright © of selection remains with the editors –
Aidan Coleman and Juliet A. Paine

All rights reserved. This book is copyright. Apart from fair dealing
for the purposes of private study, research, criticism or review,
as permitted under the Copyright Act, no part may be reproduced
without written permission. Enquiries should be addressed to
the publisher.

Cover artwork by Viv Miller, *Volcano painting*, 2005, oil, enamel, acrylic
    and pencil on canvas 180 x 150 cm. Image courtesy of the artist and
    Neon Parc, Melbourne, www.vivmiller.com
Cover design by Clinton Ellicott, Wakefield Press
Edited by Aidan Coleman and Juliet A. Paine, Friendly Street Poets Inc.
Typeset by Clinton Ellicott, Wakefield Press
Printed in Australia by Griffin Digital, Adelaide

ISBN 978 1 86254 842 8

Government
of South Australia

Arts SA

Friendly Street Poets Inc. is supported
by the **South Australian Government**
through **Arts SA**.

fox creek
wines

CONTENTS

Thank you
to all the poets who read and submitted material for the book
and equally the enthusiastic, supportive audience
for actively listening.
It is this reciprocal relationship
that is the dynamic force
that feeds Friendly Street.

Thank you
for the continuing support of Arts SA
who keep our publishing program financially viable.

ACKNOWLEDGEMENT

Friendly Street Poets acknowledges the Kaurna people
as the original owners and custodians of the Adelaide Plains

PREFACE

Friendly Street Poets meet on the first Tuesday of every month at the SA Writers' Centre on Rundle Street. In 2008, additional readings were held at Port Noarlunga, Salisbury and Port Augusta. What follows is our selection from over one thousand poems.

This book certainly contains all our favourite poems; but beyond this we have also sought to represent the best of Friendly Street in all its diversity: its various styles, interests and concerns.

These 98 poems offer fire, snow and apes, seedy moths and hens with a penchant for Mozart; bees and babes and babies (occasionally edible), steroids, speed and lyrca, ESL and the CIA and a lone black-clad figure called Chainsaw; there's home economics, microeconomics and astrophysics, the most affirming haiku ever written and an idea for our national flag that will make even photocopying a patriotic activity.

We hope you find the ordinary strange and the mystery of life readable.

Aidan Coleman & Juliet A. Paine

FIRE

Hot breath fans the trees –
flames leap, somersault and spin
high on a trapeze.

*

A sheen glistens on your skin.

The oil and spice of your body,
aromatic as eucalyptus leaves,

curls my nostrils,
tastes pungent on my tongue.

When the heat comes embracing
will you too explode into flame?

*

You speak of flames – the sparking touch
on skin, fire in your veins.

I moisten your lips with mine,
pour the waters of my mouth over you,

bathe your thighs, your limbs.
You drink. I evaporate.

DAVID ADÈS

WINNING THE LOTTERY

Our first ticket
and all our numbers came in.

Of all the children
we could have conceived
it was you who came

and we will count our riches
for the rest of our lives.

DAVID ADÈS

AT SANTIAGO AIRPORT

I flew from Adelaide to Santiago
overtaking the world's turn
chasing last night, chasing the dawn
reaching into yesterday
to find an older, other version of myself
tired and in need of sleep
waiting for my arrival.

DAVID ADÈS

TETHERED

Tethered like balloon or kite
anxious to depart, Black Hill
crooked as the lip of my Pa's spade
leavers into feathered cloud,

Cloud, a slow migration of geese;
a flock as thick as industrial smog
but light at the edges as a magician's
silk handkerchief,

Handkerchief, which glides
above terracotta and the plumb
and apricot trees of my neighbour;
draped with net,

Net, strung between branches;
filled by the abra cadabra and kalamazoo
of rosella and kookaburra
who frequent cedar,

Cedar, which towers above my house;
and dives as a man head first from undergrowth;
two arms extend from belly into canopy
intricate as artery and capillary

Capillary, mirrored by the spreading afro
of root which trails from hip bone
deep into dirt where boot against spade
I dig a hole the size of small cage;

Cage, I tell my son who stands beside me
is no place for a bird, no matter how small;
this ritual one of many I suppose in the cycle
of father and son;

Son, you listened as we talked of death
watching the last breath and when I said
It would be better this way you agreed
shadowing my words;

Words, incandescent particles slippery as trout
in mountain stream, helix and solidify as bulb of light
guiding trekkers home in snow drift thick as cloud
on trails which wind and pool above tree line.

GAETANO AIELLO

THE FLY AND I

Today
I found myself making an "I" statement to a fly
as it crawled around the rim of my cup.
"Please leave" I cried with a wave of my hand
"I feel very irritated when I see your feet where I sup.
I'd like you to leave."
Said a voice from within with a breathy sigh,
"You can't negotiate with a fly"
I know this is true but still I try
even though the power of beginning with "I"
is largely lost on those I love
and words to a fly
merely buzz.

KATE ALDER

IN AACHEN CATHEDRAL

In that high gothic choir appended to
the octagon (the hallowed chapel built
by Charlemagne) black habited he stood

conversing with a lass of twenty years
perhaps, weight mainly born by firmly planted
left foot, the right foot lightly resting on

the sanctuary step, knee slightly bent
to drape the habit handsomely, and (who knows?)
allow the sack to hang and cool in comfort.

Though words were doubtless lofty, the young man's stance
projected just a little more than liking.

MURRAY ALFREDSON

INSPIRED BY THE STATUE OF LIBERTY

Oh marble goddess
Standing erect like a gallows,

It is not a torch of liberty you carry!

Lower your arm!
For the Pentagon sees it a torch
To burn the fields of the world with.

And the CIA see it a sword
To behead all those who do not bow
To the gods of the "White Temple".

There are steel helmets
That should be shoes for the barefooted,
And there are shoes
That can helmet the heads of generals
Who won't stop arming hatred
Against love,
And leaders
Who strangle the world
And tune their global anthem
To the screams of children
And the cries of the wretched.

I can almost believe
That God loves a worshiper
As much as he hates the gods of the
White House!

I can almost believe
That hell starts
In the lobbies of the Pentagon!

I can almost believe
That the CIA is the devil's den!

I need a rope
That stretches from Hiroshima to Baghdad
To air the clothes of the children
Drenched in their blood.

I need another rope
To stretch from Nagasaki to Alfalouja,
From Fanoom banah to the holy Najaf
To air the clothes of the loss struck mothers
Whose children's lives were the harvest
Of the Pentagon scythe.

And another rope
To stretch from Havana to Santiago
To air the pages of the black books
About the American cowboy
Leading his steel herds
To spread bloody-mocracy
Around the globe.

I need Holaco's heart
To taste the victory
Of the American liberator
After he raped that Eden flower:
Abir Qasem Hamza,
Before he embroidered her chest
With his bullets
And set the soft bodies afire
To thaw the frost still in his veins.

Whatever the miseries yet to come
Whatever the wrath of volcanoes and high rains
And the destruction they could leave behind,
The generations of tomorrow
Will surely be better than ours
For one sole reason:
Tomorrow there will not be
A dragon named:
George Bush the grandson.

YAHIA AL-SAMAWY

BACK GATES

Sixties houses had secret passages
to neighbours, tucked in leafy corners:
from a loose sheet of tin
making music in the wind
to a welded pipe-gate,
fully hinged and tightly sprung.

Most swung free, though some
were overgrown with vines, rusted shut,
or chained over a festering quibble.
Some were overused: that certain
squeak that said, "She's back!" –
the cringe at footsteps on the porch.

As kids, we loved our synapse in the steel,
hoicked bikes and toys over the bar.
Later, as gangly teenagers, leaning at this
low point, we chatted to boys next door.
Our dogs thrust paws through latch holes
and nuzzled snout to snout underneath.

These days, few know the comfort
of this back fence bond, this odd pail missing,
that says "trust". With daily headlines
of thieves and fierce times,
there's no tin-kettlings in the burbs –
and no-one runs out of sugar.

JUDE AQUILINA

MOTH
Agrotis infusa

I am the plain, hairy cousin
of that graceful, gaudy show-off.
I'm out on the town, while she's
fast asleep. I stop at the first
lit window, soliciting other night-life.
I fling myself at the seamy element:
anything hot and white.
The moon is a sleazy pimp
spurning this orgy under a public lamp.
I whirl in frenzied circles with the mob,
my dress a torn mess,
I'm dizzy and drunk on light.

JUDE AQUILINA

MORNING HEAVES HERSELF ...

Morning heaves herself
over the hilltop
spills into day.

MAEVE ARCHIBALD

REAL

It's only real if it happens in California.
Brushing biscuit crumbs slowly from her dress,
she observes the flicker of lives across the screen.
This room is cosy, if a little cramped.

Brushing biscuit crumbs slowly from her dress,
she watches the nightly show from across the planet.
This room is cosy, if a little cramped.
Wind howls around the corner of the building.

Watching the nightly show from across the planet,
carefully she dons her pyjamas, creeps into bed.
Wind howls around the corner of the building.
Her radio is handy if sleep fails.

Carefully she dons her pyjamas, creeps into bed,
as the U.S. President denounces the axis of evil.
Her radio is handy if sleep fails;
music on the FM station is relaxing.

The U.S. President denounces the axis of evil.
The nurse will bring fresh tablets in the morning.
Music on the FM station is relaxing.
A handful of rain flings at the closed window.

The nurse will bring fresh tablets in the morning.
She observes the flicker of lives across the screen.
A handful of rain flings at the closed window.
It's only real if it happens in California.

LYNETTE ARDEN

JONAH

Somewhere in the crumpled night, playing
with black, the restless ocean sways
to the whale's long croon and sigh.
And Jonah lifts up his voice from a deep
where neither fluke nor fin lets light between
the sea-foamed clefs, and dark of seaweed staves
curling about the fat and oily song of sleep.

From below the knock of rocking hulls he calls,
lost, beneath the sea's sly susurrations; stays
at sleep-estuary's soft-fingered edge, wanting
the near-knowings that he cannot keep,
where all dreamers' eyes, sliding open, weep
for the half-seen, shell-sharp secrets of themselves.
"Oh Lord, why must I go to Nineveh? Why me?"

HENRY ASHLEY-BROWN

THE SWARM OF BEES

They speak – erratically –
forgetfully, remembering
a story, a task,
about swarming,
like binary codes
shaggy with humming.
One brushes my lips.
Ones and zeroes
gather disquieted
And I, also programmed,
wave my arms about
my head, then stop.
Older vestiges resonate
tamed by the thought
of honey.

HENRY ASHLEY-BROWN

BONES OF THE LAND

(The Breakaway Hills)

You can sure see the bones of the land from up here:
like that long time ago when the sea was freezing cold –
the old people still sing and croon at sunset,

a mouthful of sand and bristling wind
the window sky's just a strange leadlight –
and you can sure see the bones of the land from up here.

These days, they turn the country inside out
looking for their pretty pebbles –
(the old people still sing and croon at sunset)

how strange fish swam here, turned to stone long since,
how the world has seams of hidden treasure
and you can sure see the bones of the land from up here.

Fabulous beasts glisten and turn like dreams
the rocks gossip and laugh with the wind,
the old people still sing and croon at sunset –

and the next round's on the gibber-plain
for nothing's ever finished under the wild-eyed moon,
the old people still sing and croon at sunset
and you can sure see the bones of the land from up here.

AVALANCHE

THE WILD FLOWERS

for Patti

The flowers for sale at the Willunga market
are springing haphazardly from containers
on the counter or on the ground.
There's the spiky Callistemon,
a clutch of Kangaroo Paws,
the Hakea, the Grevillea, the wan flannel flower,
the dense domed Banksia with its tattered foliage
and a burst of Waratah.
They mass like the remnants
of their Maker's imaginings
or the sketchy meanderings of a drunken hand.
They curl and hiss and growl,
hail the woman in an unknown idiom,
while her thoughts turn to her homeland,
to the passion of the carnation,
the warmth of the daisy and the gently-petalled rose.
Given a bunch of those wild flowers
at the market she'd receive them
as you'd receive an oddly-dressed foreigner,
or see them as objects from a ragtag land.
She stands back from their mean perfume
and the faint smell of gum.
Perhaps she believes that one day
she will come to accept them but not yet, not now.

ELAINE BARKER

ENGLISH AS A SECOND LANGUAGE

Where do these girls come from when they lay
flat-bellied on our hearth-rug in the soak
of cold-day heat? The fizzling television
muted flames. What are they dreaming of?
They're nice enough. Just up to the usual things
we're all young once. They come from broken homes.
Their nice hard-working mothers, briefly met
work double-time. Keep boyfriends of their own.

Are these girls our boys' girlfriends? Who could say?
When are their mothers home? Best not to ask.
They catch the bus. They're only renting here.
We catch them out. They know to pull apart
when they hear footsteps coming near the room.
They're nice enough. Though no-one's nice enough
for our boys really. Still, we're all young once.

They clump around together in a rush
these girls explore boys' bedrooms like museums
the dens we mothers curate, knowing that
curators cannot guess at secret dreams.
Dust the scrolls as often as you like
it won't teach you to read the hieroglyphs.

These are not the sorts of girls we mothers
would garland with the words *stunning* or *striking*
their awkward standing-pose their elbow-scratching
curving bend, a question mark that knows.
Vaguely-coloured eyes. Wet mouth that drawls
and nearly, but not quite, gives lisp to s

but nice enough. So would you like to stay
an hour more for dinner as our guest?

It's casserole. These mothers nice enough
are sometimes out but often home. We talk
but sometimes with your teeth there in his neck
do you feel your Transylvanian second tongue?
Or where do these thoughts come from? When we lay
skin copper-warm. His parents, for once, not home?

Secrets kept by drawers. Wardrobes and boxes
notebooks photo albums dog-toothed smiles
are maddening as the teeth there in your neck –
but keep them there. Don't stop. And no, not yet.
There's no need now. The footsteps in retreat.
Act natural-like. He doesn't have to know
that you hang upside down at night to sleep.

Who knows which way is up here, when he sleeps alone?

COURTNEY BLACK

EVERGREEN

They have cut down the tree,
the evergreen that flourished
like an everlasting line from Psalms.

They are chanting a mantra
as they carry our shade, our refuge away,
Stratco, Stratco, Stratco.

KAREN BLAYLOCK

LAMENTATIONS

Today, I have happiness in-house,
the rose flowering yellow by the window,
light stepping through the door,
birds are maestros singing all is well
and all manner of things shall be well;
wind and trees, the altos, join the fray.

There is no talk of weather in the skies,
no prophecies in clouds,
no tomorrow in the frequencies of hours,
and yet it comes, the morning, no surprise,
like a book of Lamentations,
Ah – renew our days of gold.

KAREN BLAYLOCK

KEEPSAKES

The legs leaned against each other in the corner of the cupboard,
as if they were a little band of runners who rested there in order
to regain their strength before continuing the journey . . .

Alex Miller in *Landscape of Farewell*

Years before I was born,
my mother cut off and sold
her long dark plaits.
They were so long she could sit on them.
She wanted a thirties '*bob*'
so in defiance of her mother's wishes
she severed the maternal strands with scissors.
As a child I remember a photo
which hung in the passage-way
of my grandparent's house. A photo
of a girl with a fringe and long dark plaits.

My uncle had no photos of himself,
never spoke of '*the accident*'
but kept a collection of his wooden legs
in a cupboard under the stairs.
They ranged in size through boyhood
into manhood. Like best friends
they had walked each day
the same dry and dusty road to school,
had scuffed their boots kicking the limestone,
were both exempt from war service.

It is said that when women want to rebel
the first thing they do is to cut off their hair.
How many years does it take
for hair to grow until, when plaited,
you can sit on the smooth dark ropes of it?
Was my mother paid by weight or length?
I wish she had kept her plaits.
I like the thought of keeping them in a drawer,
carefully folded into a silk scarf,
blue I think, to match the colour of her eyes.

MARY BRADLEY

LADY CHAT

Lady Chat. Lady Chat. I'd love a bit of all that.
Better than Hire a Hubby.
I thought of you the other day
when I strolled in the back yard.
The glory vine was out of control,
growing over the barbecue.
The pergola was on a lean and
as for the shed,
Angels fear to tread.
Now if I had a live-in gardener
we could plant the sunflowers and
water the cherry tomatoes too,
grow a few herbs, chilli, garlic in pots and
I would love a yacca plant.
Lady Chat, I could do with that,
and having done the weeding and mowing
we could drink cups of tea,
surrounded by the bougainvillea spilling over the wall.
Lady Chat, if I had all that,
The happy plant on my veranda would never wilt and die.

KATE BRISTOW

EXIT ROW

you've been allocated
a seat
on exit row

you resist
the gravitational
pull

the desire
to rip the door out
at 30,000 feet

instead
you settle
for a bottle of red

& make the most
of the extra
        leg
           room

STEVE BROCK

FAIR GO

for Ervin

When I was logging
there was a bloke there called Bill.
He used to grab me by the hair
and pull me round saying,
"Look! I got myself a wog here."
I was fair game he reckoned
because I'm short. I was under
this bloody oaf's hand saying,
"Let me go, you prick, it hurts."
And he's saying, "Oh, listen to the wog.
'It hurts, it hurts.'"
But he hadn't got the measure of me,
and next thing he was on the ground
with a broken wrist, crying like a baby.
I wasn't brought up on the streets
for nothing, but I thought, *I'm dead.*
All his friends were standing round
and they were bigger than him.
So I'm looking round like a cornered dog,
but not one of them moved.
He deserved it, they reckoned.
Fair go, they reckoned.

BELINDA BROUGHTON

FIG LEAVES

Adam's belly was tight with seriousness and blind faith.
He knew nothing of sensual delights or even animal instinct.
He was on his rock waiting for God I think.
He was lean with fasting. Meanwhile I was retching
on my desire and curiosity, growing thin
on stars and water. I wanted words and ideas,
vivid opinions, something more interesting
than the garden. Then I met the serpent.
He understood my predicament and boredom.
He shared with me some secrets he'd learnt
when he was in God's good books –
that there is so much more and we can *know* it.
"Well," I thought, "I've had enough of basking
on lawns all day. Give me some stimulation."
So I enticed Adam down from his rock
and we shared a bit of knowledge.
I'd been so used to him hanging around on rocks
that I hadn't even noticed his superb body.
The sex we had was so intense it was embarrassing,
hence the fig leaves, besides which later
we could strip them off each other.
God heard our moans. That's what woke him up.
He didn't have a lot to say because he was so jealous
but he cast us out of his paradise into the rest of his creation.
Out here there is this minor problem of death
but the sex is still good.

BELINDA BROUGHTON

THE TROUBLE FOR LILLITH

Did you know God took away
nine-tenths of women's love
so they would not eat their babies?
You know why: such cute little seraphim legs,
heads soft on lips, liquid nowhere eyes.

The trouble for Lillith was
God didn't take it from her –
for the care of the babies you understand.
She was such a magnificent protectress
a she-wolf at the den door.

It was ok when she had someone to hate,
but once the danger was over, oh those babies,
how they smelt with their milk breath,
their sugar-coated plump little hands,
their firm peachy bottoms.

She got the taste for it;
one does they say.
And after her ardent attentions,
there wasn't much left:
a few bones, some gristly ears.

BELINDA BROUGHTON

NEW YORK

We were leaving
an afternoon
of coloured glass and temples:

your gloved hand
snug
in my gloved hand.

The sky was later than you'd think.
The way it would have been
when Wallace Stevens wrote his poem.

Giant TVs
had fallen to earth
and neon bubbled hot through pipes.

New Yorkers were hurrying home, dressed
in hats and scarves and cheerful
optimism.

I think we were talking pizza, when
a snow began –
so delicate

it might have been
falling
skyward.

AIDAN COLEMAN

WHY OLD LADIES HAVE POT PLANTS

they used to have gardens,   big gardens
full of children and dogs and cats
now they have narrow strips of sunless earth between fences
and no pets.

by order.

so now they have pot plants;
odd pots, odd plants, different sizes, clashing styles and colours:
they need a lot of looking after

just like children.

Old gentlemen had better not interfere with old ladies' pot plants
(if they know what's good for them).

beware.

BETTY COLLINS

HAIKU

perched on power line staves
small birds sing
the notes they form

DAWN COLSEY

SMALL TOWN SATURDAY

A brown dog sniffs at Main Street
where Monday chafes behind glass.
Bowlers mill like termites
around the hem of their green,
ignore Saint Peter's choir rehearsing Handel.
Rusting iron fences echo my footfall,
the past sits on verandahs with old men
and the breeze is frying onions.

DAVID COOKSON

POISED ON MOSS

poised on moss
pearls of dew, hesitate
to start their journey

DOROTHY CORMACK

AIR FARE

On the plane
I ate
an airline meal
with a metal fork
and a plastic knife
from a number of containers
which needed to be
de-lidded
and half a dozen sachets
that needed to be
ripped open
and three cups for liquid
that were best
not spilt
and some tin-foil
which had to be
peeled off
while I had
someone else's elbow
on my plate
and a pillow
between my knees
and a handbag
beneath my feet
and a blow up neck rest
around my thigh
and a set of headphones
over my ears
and a remote control
resting on my stomach
and a seat belt
around my waist

It tasted
complicated

JUDY DALLY

I AM A BOARDING HOUSE

with everyday regulars
who pay their weekly rent   on time
wipe clean their window sill, hand basin
tut-tut the neighbour who doesn't
who lets the wastepaper basket overflow

perhaps there's a caretaker who's part of this
psyche-cast   he's the one who
when the prettiest girl is bathing
creeps up to the cardboard door
peeps through its tiny keyhole

after dark others emerge
unsavoury, long-term lodgers
who've made it their business
never to greet the new arrivals
they are the basement dwellers
or, the penthouse ones

surely the landlady's in on it
oh yes, I know she's me, too
that jolly Frau who'd angle a favour-in-lieu
as long as the tenant were good enough
                                    and hot enough
to give what she could ask for

there's loads of material for a play
a TV series, maybe   if only I could stand
the constant squabbling
all of them auditioning
for the lead

KATE DELLER-EVANS

A NEW FLAG

It's time to debate our national flag.
It's time to roll up the colonial rag.
       To-day they expect us to salute the Southern Cross.
       Tomorrow we'll be free to douse it in petrol and toss
A match at our obsolete emblematic tag.

It's time to devise a new symbol for the nation
To rally us in war with a blaze of ostentation.
       Would Diggers rush to die under an Aboriginal banner?
       Well, I have a suggestion based on the military manner.
I propose a flag with a field completely white.

No design, no cross, no star, just a field of white –
To evoke perpetual surrender, reluctance to fight,
       Unity, universality, purity of driven snow,
       Every colour and hue blending in a harmonious flow
       Towards the core of a star's effulgent glow.

We'll carry a standard of white as we march to war.
       The enemy, thinking we're surrendering, will hold their fire.
Australians, whenever they feed their printers a blank A4,
       Will be seized with patriotic sentiment, which should inspire
Pride of nationality, suffused with white light –
Enough, perhaps, to widen the narrow, tight
       Group identity, lifting standards standards higher.

Paper without imprints deserves salutes.
       Next to borderless territory for which it stands,
       Pride of lineage, vain attachment to native lands,
And suspiciously motivated international disputes
Seem primitive, jealous and selfish, petty pursuits.

The United Nations flag is on the right track:
  Patches of white in a pale blue field
So let's cut out the union jack,
  And join the stars by removing the background of blue,
  For then the nuclear fusion of all life
Shall be emblazoned in glory on our new, shining shield.

K. NIGEL DEY

VESTIGES

Caught in idle cobwebs
feather, insect, leaf
a collage
waiting
to be brushed away
like totems
crushed in swathes
remnants
cling to bristles
as though
defiant.

GENNY DREW

SONNET TO LOST INNOCENCE

The Beatles wrote they'd kiss and be so true,
Sinatra crooned of love and adoration.
Connie sang with soul, "My heart loves you",
Streisand sighed of love as liberation.
"All you need is love", another cry
of lyrics sung with promised, heartfelt truth.
Love always would be there and never die
in a world that promised coloured dreams to youth.
Now the words are angry, sick and crude,
the lyrics violent, full of hurt and pain.
The rapper screams he'll fuck the naked prude,
she's just a red-haired bitch, a permed plain Jane.
Songs of today bleed with indifference,
the old lie's best, despite lost innocence.

TESS DRIVER

REVELATIONS AT THE BUS STOP

Bus stop 19. We are waiting,
together, silent, strangers.
The girl is still, her eyes are wild.
I see the bruise too big for a love bite,
black purple against pale skin,
her coat too thin for the cold.

"Bit nippy", I smile.
The bundle in her arms whimpers.
 "Cold for the bub. How old?"
She turns to me, a face too hard and closed
in a seventeen year old body.
"Six days. Baby cried. He said he'd drop it
if it didn't shut up.
I'm going to my Mum's."

No tears. Just facts.
We hail the 369,
I help her load her life on board.

TESS DRIVER

FOR STRETCH

Desperate whimpers greet you from their derelict concrete dens
Occupied only by unwanted blankets and a water dish
Brown eyes unblinking almost as if without hope
Placid compared to other neglected gallow dwellers
Violently replicating the mistreatment they were bestowed
Ribcages evident, lampshade necklaces adorned
To resist him from chewing at the already depleted frame
Deformed features due to bad breeding prove to be the final crux
Barely standing on deformed paws
Supported by weak legs and diminished appetite
He gazes at me with almost hollow optimism
But as my eyes water he intuitively slumps again
He knows that I cannot retrieve him
Further accepting life "on the farm"
I just hope he knows how hard it was to walk away

ANDREW ELLERY

SONNET FOR A SUICIDE

Inspired by Robert Pinsky

Morning sun on his face
steady motor murmur
vibrating the hose

Bluebells clamber
over the hill's top –
nothing to remember

only the same engine noise
that keeps making the same sounds
under his head poised

and pulsing the same beat
no-one to say his name,
no need, no-one to praise him,

only the engine's voice – over
and over, running under him.

M. L. EMMETT

FEMINISM'S BABES

Young women know all about style –
how to fix the decimal point
between them and their mothers
differentiate themselves
from Special K over 40s wanna bees
mini skirted and high heeled
trying to catch their husband's eye

Yummy mummies in their 30s
are separated from the new stock
by firm elastic flattened midriffs
that do not bulge or wobble
unlined skin taut sometimes
navel pierced or nipples
their legs wear the 4" heels again
on winkle-pickered pointed toes
for a mid-century crop
of bunioned feet.

No scraggy necks or waddle
no tea tray arses only
plump peaches
in the bend over show
of skimpy, lacy thongs
of rectal floss

So, sexy femme fatale is cool
body object the thing to be
flouncing and preening
flirting and fucking
random hook-ups on the run
in the alleys of time on the net
in the warp of space
Killer! Whatever!
Wicked! Feral!

M. L. EMMETT

STEROIDS, SPEED & LYCRA

Le Tour de France 2007

A lush of Lycra
wrapped tight
round bulked thighs
curled backs
and crotches of little promise
lime green striped
cobalt and electric blues
hot pink contrasting black
Lycra wet and sticky
in the European sun.

From behind
high saddles firmly lodged
in tight-arsed cracks
bright buttocks like moons
contrast with sponsored messages:
Lotto, Liquigas, Quickstep,
and *Predictor Mobil*

Comma shaped helmets
aerodynamic warrior wear
science and design
so ridiculous to the casual eye
that cannot see the do or die
of the teams so sleek
and sponsor strategic
their lives and fortunes
all ride
on this.

M. L. EMMETT

CHAINSAW AT WRITERS' WEEK
Adelaide 2008

Chainsaw Prepares

Before leaving his hotel,
Chainsaw bends to pray.
He calls down the glory of the word.
He calls down stutters
and bad reviews
on his bitter rivals,
wherever they may be.
Chainsaw stands.
He is ready.

Chainsaw Arrives

Chainsaw in his funereal suit
goes looking for a fight.
Angry in black he ponders a sea of chairs,
a landscape without poetry
or heroic figures,
and strikes a pastoral pose,
hoping to be recognised.

But Chainsaw's lost his mojo.
His black-cat bone is in his other jacket
and his rhymes are out of sorts,
so he makes notes for his biography instead
and waits his moment,
the summons to the altar.

Chainsaw Reads

Chainsaw on the podium
reads the poem very loudly –
fast as a race call,
fast as an auctioneer's song.
Like a nail gun set on automatic.

Chainsaw gets his teeth in.
He's incandescent and sprinting now,
tripping over the words,
forgetting to breathe,
right into his furious stride and swing,
seeing the finishing line ahead.

Then it's the dead end he loves,
the sweet stop
at the last of it
when his chain rests
before the perfect
ruins of his work –
his holy, holy work.

Chainsaw Reflects

Chainsaw plays guitars to splinters,
and has doomed affairs with lovers
who will never write as well as he can.
He loves stories with chainsaws in them,
and women's dresses too
because, as he always says,
he's a romantic at heart.

Chainsaw once had a wooden hut to live in but ate it.
Even knowing he would be unsheltered,
he could not help himself.
He is exposed here,
but in his pocket is a map of the world
with his birthplace circled in red.
It comforts him.

Chainsaw doesn't believe in any religion except death
and he's working towards that with unswerving faith.
He knows he speaks the one true language.
The book of Chainsaw's life is being written on ice.
No-one else can claim that.

Chainsaw Leaves

Afterwards there are
the empty tent, the empty chairs,
and the litter of plastic cups
in the place where he spoke.

One last look over his shoulder
before he hoists the aching lines he must carry,
setting out for the next chapter
in the story of Chainsaw.

STEVE EVANS

A PIANIST'S HANDS

I knew my grandfather
from a distance.
He was a quiet man
his words stayed folded
like a letter never opened.
Only once do I remember
his words to me.
I was twelve.
He asked
if I played the piano
said my fingers
were long and slender
like the pianist at his church.
I stayed silent
scared to cover his words
with mine.
I wanted to photograph them
frame them in my mind
hold them as a reminder
of all the words
he might have said to me
if someone had opened
the letter.

JOAN FENNEY

ALEXANDER AND THE RAIN

Alexander, aged one,
sees the water falling from the clouds
silver-grey onto the wooden table
turning red-brown in the rain,
sees the rain
deepen the red of paving bricks,
stretches out his little hand
to touch the water pools
forming under the drain pipe

He has as yet
no words for colour.

MARGARET FENSOM

DUBAI PASSÉ

A hotel set to sail, a marlin
caught in a jpeg file.
The material of language
revealing more than glass and steel.
An addiction to sweet tea
and the syrup of foreign currency.
Western brands in Arabic curves.
A trace of authentic dust
sunk in salt marsh.
A desert-ocean hybrid:
the blurring sand, the merging
genres of water and land.
Building islands and a golf course
with a mirage of Bedouin
tents at the seventeenth green.
From all angles,
a mélange of cultures
consumed like a daiquiri
with miniature umbrella
by the rising surf
of a tidal pool.

CAMERON FULLER

THE 'NUKE-U-LAR' FAMILY
March 2003

Balloons pop before the party begins,
but still they entertain the idea of one inflated
piece of rubber for each year of life.
All generations under one veranda
coughing on the smoke of burning meat.

Amid deckchairs and eskies, tomato sauce and grease soak
through paper plates and stain summer dresses.
Singing to the radio, active kids dance and lean
into air microphones. Time implodes in the sun
until a news broadcast interrupts with the boom

of an announcer's voice. Then that party animal-
turned-President of the World drops
'nuke-u-lar' down the airwaves.
The extra syllable is not lost in the backyard.
In-laws argue about expressions of power.

Another war lies ahead and meanings are not new or clear.
To some people an axis of evil sounds *cool*.
"I'm a rogue nation", a boy yells as he runs in circles and,
full with chops and fizzy drinks, pukes on grass.
The sugar-fuelled surge is over in seconds

but fallout remains. Behind the grin of harmless fun
other hazards appear. When handled while drunk
barbeque tongs are offensive weapons.
A water pistol in the wrong hands and everyone
gets soaked. The children launch a farting contest

and adults start to worry about the wind direction.
Somehow there is no emotional meltdown.
As dusk arrives, the tables are cleared of bones
and fairy bread crusts. The hundreds and thousands spilt
on the ground will be swept up in tomorrow's light.

Before the moon, the family is dispersed across a city.
One year older but asleep already, a child breathes
in relative silence, unaware that memories
made and buried in backyards
will one day resurface.

The present   disintegrates into atoms.

CAMERON FULLER

WINDOW SEATS

It always has struck me as odd
that the cabin crew so diligently show us
how to use a life vest, when the whole flight
is over land, with barely enough water to catch
a geometer's reflections of the tracking sun.
But as we cross the equator, eight miles
above the breaking swells of the Pacific Ocean,
for once, it doesn't seem such a bad idea.

From the vapid smell-drift of sleep and coffee,
a faint scent of familiarity envelops my allocated space.
Naturally, I recognise it is not yours.
(How much do they sell in a year of duty free?)
In any case, the curling tendrils of perfume
draw me out of my seat and closer to home,
to streets lined purple with November jacarandas,
to our shared, all-embracing air.

IAN GIBBINS

MAKING JAM

Just look at the apricot tree today,
all those golden orbs lying in
the lap of the sun, soaking it up.
See how, when I reach out to pluck
the sunset of those fruits
they blush, coy and seductive,
at the touch of my hand.

Tomorrow they'll unfold the fragrance
of their flesh until their perfume
webs each corner of the house
in joyful expectation
knowing that when winter comes
each time we open up a jar
their summer sun will fill the room.

JILL GLOYNE

GARDEN JEWELS

in spring she plants them
tiny leaves in tiny pots
they look lost in the brown earth
of the veggie patch
that has been dug and hoed
and smoothed in preparation

in spring they start to grow
new shoots sprout and leaves expand
soon they must be tied to stakes
green basil sweet beneath them
to fight off the invasion of insects
before long small green tomatoes
appear between the foliage

she watches the summer sun do its work
as it turns the tiny round tomatoes scarlet
others are miniature pear-shaped fruit
that she picks and stuffs straight into her mouth
popping the skins with her teeth
the sweetness exploding against her tongue

today's harvest waits in a wooden bowl
and against the mellow timber hues
they look like shiny red beads
waiting to be threaded
and worn to celebrate sunny days

but she has a better plan
for these jewels of sweetness
she will scatter them
over crisp cos and creamy goats cheese
drizzle with olive oil and eat with crusty bread
on this lazy summer's afternoon

JILL GOWER

GRANDMOTHER, GARDEN

if your hand
was the brown
smooth grease of clay
& after holding it in mine
i would have this impression
of the faraway country
behind your eyes & i would carry
this back to the house i share with
your daughter who i married
twenty years ago & say
to her & your grand daughters
this is a part of you
& place it where it would
catch the sun
& then a week later
return to hold your hand
& again collect
the impression
that in other circumstances
when broken down
with a little sand
to turn silty loam
& with a little water
& the craft of gardening
it could begin a life
as holding your hand firmly
in late afternoon
tea time begins mine
your eyes closed
to the television's opera
to the garden growing
inside your door

RORY HARRIS

THRESHOLDS

before i learnt to polish both
front & back steps
with dark tan shoe polish
my mother did it before me

i step through
the back door of
my father's house
avoid the step

the food i bring is not exotic
more what is eaten now
& what i remember him liking
there are always lamb chops in the freezer
cost has nothing to do with it

twin tube washing machines
went out with the permanent wave

the heels of your hands
held your whiskey glass
three was the limit
my father gave you

bargains, specials & sales
the non-stick saucepan now sticks
bought discounted thirty years ago
it was an investment

how much malice
how much memory
how much defeat

i can walk away
from the freshly weeded garden
& leave it until next year
& the next phone call

all the rusted tools are in the shed
tins of outdated dried paint

no one applies floor wax by hand
to reflect your table manners
a skidding of freshly shelled peas

you are cutting in the edges
between the walls & skirting boards
the tradesman's quote was simply too steep

RORY HARRIS

TRAILS KEPT FROM THE WIND

I've missed imagining,
Your faraway thoughts
Left in breaths of cloudy air
Disappearing from train windows

In handwriting
On the wings of paper cranes
For others to find
So their buried wishes
Might fly on the breeze,

Stained in fingerprints
Snared on book pages
Amongst graphite wonderings
And smears of dried aubergine.

In memories of struck notes
Echoing through piano keys
That open no door
And shut no mind.

MEL HUGHES

KISS

as I stood under the stars
with you
Dali's elephants kissed
the seven sisters
clocks melted over
the hills hoist
air became more spacious
I levitated
you flew up
to find me
lips touching

INDIGO

THINKING ABOUT THE 'GOLDILOCKS' PLANET

Scientists have said
our blue planet is
'Just right' for us.

But Goldilocks
came, ate, slept
broke furniture.

Today, we
might call it
home invasion.

And she left
careless of destruction
and distress.

Will she be
on the 'ship' that
leaves Earth behind?

ERICA JOLLY

GONE!

Sixteen years of dinners,
of school lunches,
of early breakfasts and
tri-weekly washing.

Sixteen years of reminders to
clean-up your room
do your homework and
eat your dinner – *please!*

Sixteen years of refereeing
of praising, guiding, arguing and
Jeez! I can't bloody wait
to have a minute's peace!

Sixteen years and they've gone
left me to my own quiet house
left me in peace – finally
to do as I please

to become the person I was
or the person I want to be
while they holiday overseas
for *three* weeks!

After sixteen years I am suspended
between silence and possibility
and in the impossible stillness
of dinner for one and a tidy house

I do nothing and become no one.

SHARON KERNOT

BLOOD WORK

As kids we bounced along
the Main North Road
through Gepps Cross
in the back of the old ute
our wind-whipped hair
sheltered by the cab
our noses pinched
and our voices squealing
at the stench of abattoir death.
Back then, a steak sandwich
or a barbequed chop
was not an animal.

Now, all that land has been scraped
blood and guts
scoured from the earth
but the soil still breathes memories
of mutilation
in a place where the stages of grief
death and dying
had no meaning to most

like the meat worker
who told of the young slaughterman
who showed her how
to shoot a bolt through the skull
of a terrified cow
and how they drank and laughed
at her party trick later
at the Meatman's pub.

When I hear the clatter of hooves
in a cattle truck
staggering at the mercy
of each grinding gear shift
I grieve for them
and for the thousands
that leave the killing stalls
and enter the slicing room
to endure amputations
of legs and tails and skin
twitching, writhing: alive.

SHARON KERNOT

UNCLE KARNO'S LAST GRUMBLE

Now listen here my child: I may be gone
Real soon, but don't forget what Uncle Karn
Has taught you through the years. And that doggone
Kid-generation 'f yours, I know their yarns
And what they see as model ideals. I
Have come to understand that they, beside
That Terrace house of government, ally
Themselves not with a peasant's outlook. "Ride
That wave of even ground!" the kids still yell.
But ah, the world's but cactus yet, with pricks
To spare, but spare it don't I hear propelled
Discussions of equality; stoic
And suited women running down the White
House. Bah! Equality will be the day
When men like you and I will feel alright
To wear high heels and skirts along the bay,
Roadway and at our women's birthdays. Lies!
It's all but lies! I've learnt enough and so
Will you. But look at me: I'm in disguise
And off to die a bitter fool – ego
Aglow with the dull black of coal – sexless
And with a wife that can't cook water. "Cos!
I'm not yet done with him my dear!" Address
Her, go, and let her know that just because
She's feeling sexy, doesn't mean she is.

ADAM KLIMKIEWICZ

LONDON UNDERGROUND

For Lorcan

Here
in the London underground
at 1am.

There are no foxes
or bats

Nor even
the scent
of a werewolf

Just
a few thousand
commuters and

A busker
whose electric guitar
has plugged us
into

The conveyer-belt
escalator

Making a late
run
for the tube

A Japanese
backpacker
squeezes in

Folding herself
up like
a map

JULES LEIGH KOCH

REPARTNERED

At fifty, he repartnered. Sylwia
was Polish. She showed him pictures
of woods surrounded by mountains.
He plumbed Europe's dark heart.

She left her old husband for him.
He left his wife when she discovered
them together in the marital bed;
to repent was too much bother.

He created memories for his new wife.
Sylwia was flattered, to start with –
they were complicit in a fairy tale,
a new history that had always been.

Their past life was in Australia,
her face, smooth skin, a dark mole,
pasted over historical heads
in sun-bleached photographs.

They had honeymooned in Uluru,
holidayed in Tasmanian forests,
renewed their vows in Daintree,
had a blue-eyed child, lost it.

No, she said. I must leave you.
Sylwia lived with a Danish woman
then a younger Romanian man
by the Black Sea, for a time.

Years later, they met by accident
at a resort in Broome. He dined
with Sylwia, their younger partners swam.
"Are you happy?" Peter asked.

"The answer is obvious," she replied.
She showed him a faded photograph
of a child. The picture, black-and-white,
contained a slash of red.

STEPHEN LAWRENCE

HAIKU

Absolutely yes.
Yes, absolutely. Yes. Yes.
Yes, oh yes. Oh, yes.

STEPHEN LAWRENCE

WASHING OUT THE WINDOW

Coloured pegs cling to the line,
obediently pinching arms and legs.

Wind flaps sails of spots,
stripes and ordinary white sheets.

Dark clouds loom.
Time to rush outside.

TANYA LEONARDO

A VALEDICTION, FORBIDDING DROOLING

*Wherein Robert Drewe's love for Stephanie Rice, swimming champion,
is considered.*

Robert Drewe, Oh Robert Drewe
What the Hell got into you?
Stephanie Rice got into her bathers
And you got into a very big lather.
In addition to the medals that she has got
She also made you lose the plot.
I realise you have a thing for water,
But come on, Bob, she could be your daughter!

PAUL LOBBAN

ON BEING COMPARED TO A GNAT

You have the attention span,
he said,
of a gnat.

I thought (briefly)
about that:

the skim
the look;
the review
not the book;

the single
not the CD;
a movement not
the whole symphony;

the single poem –
a story won't do –
especially if short
think haiku.

Life's short.
Try this, that.
Stay light,
says the gnat.

JOHN MALONE

LETTERS TO NOWHERE

Zealously yearning xylocaine whilst vainly usurping the stabbing, residual, quiet pain of neo medical lobotomies, kinesthetically juxtaposing inherently hideous, gasping fragments, emanating downward, coiling beyond apprehension.
Always bringing colour, dynamically etching foreign gilded habits in journeys, kaleidoscopically launching miniscule nuances of perfect questions, rushing sweetly to understanding voices, weaving xenial yarns zealously.

alphabetically speaking

. . . of course

mcm (MARK C MARTIN)

GUITAR

I have the body of a guitar.
When I lie down to meditate
my neck is straight
I clear my mind
of things I've fretted about
let go my strings of attachment.

My soul is a sound box
it draws in the songs of birds,
the pulsation of insects,
the gentle movement of breezes,
transforms the vibrations of nature
into meditation music.

I breathe in
breathe out
repeat the cycle
creating chords of calm
to lift me above the physical
resonating with riffs of bliss
tuned to perfection.

DEB MATTHEWS-ZOTT

UNPLUGGED

it's not quite
that
way,

I know you think I'm rude,

but it's not
that
I never answer it,

I just never plug the thing in.

horses gallop
in
the outback,

dingoes howl at the moon,

eagles seek
the
rabbit,

and I just never plug the thing in.

IAN MESSENGER

CRUCIBLE

when I was ill
and trapped in the back room
the colours of the rose you brought me
set the table alight

in a cut crystal vase
in the late afternoon
with a clawing of leaves
and rings of water and sky

the red and the yellow
forged and glowing
in two-tone petals
each brighter than each other

blazed with shape and strength
in a cold fusion
brighter than a Blake watercolour
uncovering the core

more than neon or halogen
ballooning etched or painted light
or through the last struck window
the deflating sun

DAVID MORTIMER

NO WONDER

once there was fire
a car alight burning in a side street
so intense I nearly drove off the road at the force of the fact

intenser than rain thunderstorm anger or Brueghel's colours of
    heat in snow
fire bright brighter here more real rounded flagrant in the back
    streets near the train line
than whatever half-baked errand I thought I was on
after the football before dinner weekend wheel-turning
cauterised in one glance up against

torch crucible Bunsen burner bonfire

people from front yards drawn to watch boredom wrong-footed
residents with phones shouldered angling out to catch reality
    vouchsafed
and everything else in late afternoon not noticeably incandescent
    with flame and petrol
seemed to be seen to be concealment compromised with grey

no wonder Heraclitus felt that to only rub drag break anything open
would be to find fire

DAVID MORTIMER

DOWN THIS LIFE

down down down beneath the dumb light of the drowned sea
dark as the light gone dark as the ancient black night-sky lays
down the womb of time lays down the tomb of the young
dawning black birth from the wound that is woman
spawned from the black seed that is man
co-joined them there to lie lie in the spit of the roasted sun
burned black to the core rotten apple ferment the copulate
gives rise to the squeal that is the naked thunder voice
high-pitched the squeal dying first breath tidal baying at the moon

down down down the plunder the memory torn asunder never
to remember the birth of the placenta the driven nail through the roof
of the church its steeple rising higher than god fusing the tiny brain
to forever forget the pain of the refrained moment from which hell
burst open its bilious breach-egg the blood in the yoke
the eye of terror the taste of bad sperm the knowledge forever
hidden deep in the stairs of the mind leading in only in in situ
never flowing never yielding always blocking the stream chocking
    the dam
with silt in the mouth at the estuary of the voice no sound

down down down gargle of foetus in womb leaking tainted
    umbilical fluid
sad sad of generational purge to the new born its dowry head to tail
spinning on an axis frail as the skin breaking around cracking
    pelvic bone
out-stretched as the head tries to enter out forcing back in the wind
& the suck of the universal vacuum the big band no more than
    a whimper
the sound no more than a stone speaking a giant oyster grinding a
    tiny pearl
the diver having dived dives no more dives again the secret plaster
    alabaster
spat ammonia spit to turn & burn again & again the waiting
    wandering octopus
tentacles of ovum beginning at end & ending at birth's ferocious
    blinding blight

down down down from which you come may never you back again
lost in the world of pharaoh's slave back backed orphan of
the doomed
pray to god not of your image but effigy of a blind man with holes in
his eyelids
pray for goodness & righteousness lip service to a book printed
with blood
in the ink a squid smelling foul ejaculating be-decked throes of death
in reach of the light of life but curling with breathe that is
forsaken doom
impending following you to the furnace the cauldron from whence
you came
the lion's mane licked with the tongue of the fresh kill already rotting
in the spill
that is your life though the darkness shroud of the fluorescent cross
that beckons

down down down upwards from the ocean ground your last &
first bearing
from which you can never deviate or alternate save in a spiral fused
& welded
from conception to rigor mortis your chart is impregnated with
indelible metal
your cross to bear is the cross of the forced fuge a requiem for
the sinner
who has never sinned but is broken crippled back mouse in a trap for
that taking
the took the thief with no hands whose crime is born the hung jesus
spooking
down the leadlit filtered light the mausoleum of the devoted glued
palms praying
your salvation before your salve in the ocean deeper than the sun's
dead rays
his your first day breath you are already dead the core of this Christ
oceanic-earth is ill.

GLEN MURDOCH

AFTER LIFE

tonight the lilies in our garden
turn their pale skins to the moon

they are cupped hands
holding this fragile night

I see them through the window
glowing delicate and still

transient as the after life that bleeds
from me this fragile night

MOLLY MURN

NEW MOON

the sound of your hand
along my cheek
swells in our ears

a new moon again –
I've waxed and waned
borne noisy fruit

foot flexed against calf
hip grazing thigh
we find every slope and turn

or you cradle me –
bone weary

MOLLY MURN

ADHA CHANDRASANA

in yoga class a candle burns
for the passing of a life

last week he was beside me
doing adha chandrasana

now he is everywhere:

in the drumming rain,
beating out time

in the graceful asymmetry
of the half moon

and in the steam on the windows
from so much hot breath

MOLLY MURN

BIRD AT THE EDGE

Into the labyrinthine dip and curl
of our coffee-shop conversation –
your philandering husband, my senescent mother,
the high price of housing, the low line of televangelism –

comes a sparrow
which hops at the edge of our despair
until it charms an opening, a parting of the waters,
then taking its fill of pear and ginger cake-crumbs,

flies away,
and returns with the gift of a single feather,
as if to remind us that sometimes
what goes around comes around by the very next post

and that even the marketing crassness
of *Buy Jesus, get Moses free*
can shed a little lightness of being
on this otherwise deluded and doltish Sunday.

LOUISE NICHOLAS

THE BROWN-EYED BOY

Down a long hallway, beyond the rational mind,
is a room with your name on it. You open the door
and go in. It's all there: in a row, the houses you lived in
and those who lived there with you,
the beds you slept in and those where sleep wouldn't come,
the people next door, your teachers and school friends,
the brown-eyed boy who taught you to dance,
the way he held you, looked at you, the inexplicable stirrings,
warm and wet like the sun on the sea. It's all there.

The blue-eyed blonde with the circumstantial breasts
who fainted during assembly, the tall and handsome
maths teacher who scooped her up,
the dress you tore on a low-hanging branch
when you turned back for one last look
at the brown-eyed boy who was turning back for one last look
at the circumstantial breasts, who fainted at will
so the tall and handsome maths teacher would scoop them up
and risk dismissal one more time. It's all there.

And sometimes you wish it wasn't;
that the houses you lived in could be traded in
for the house in the woods you really wanted;
that the people next door hadn't moved away;
that the tall and handsome maths teacher
would scoop up the blue-eyed circumstance
and carry her away to the dingy cell of his own memories
and leave you alone with the brown-eyed boy for one last turn
round creaking boards at the youth club hall on a Saturday night.

LOUISE NICHOLAS

PAST MISTAKES

an iron roof peeling   like cracked sunburnt skin
creaking joints of wood
            that complain as much as arthritic knees
when hot gusts of summer wind
            blow through the farmyard
swinging the rusted gate
            that's been left   unlatched   again

creeping into the gloom
denied shadows   that have snared mystery & danger
within the infantile trap of a child's mind

in amongst
            work benches spread with bent nails & wires
            used paint brushes made from knackery waste
            serpentine sluggish old chains
                    & the unkind beaks of secateurs

it's found
            old jerry cans of petrol
            fumes intoxicating
                    overpowering dust   & ramshackle disrepair

does this child dare?
            one sniff to see   a sharp intake of breath
then an oily darkness floods with a gush
            through consciousness & sense
                    shed & daylight slip past
                                    too fast to grab

then slap   slap
            a voice demanding   *Wake up!*
You fainted!   *Don't do that again!*
            & the nausea   spinning   tumbling
for forty-eight hours non-stop.

JULIET A. PAINE

ON THE SURFACE

Snow falls like insults
on the water.

Ripples spread.
White ice turns clear,
melts,
ripples disappear.

More snow:
the surface thickens,
a little cloudy,
still smooth,
almost.

Below the surface,
it gets colder.

MICHAEL REYNOLDS

EMMA ON A RAINY DAY

It's not raining now but I'm standing
just out of the rain here above the pine trees
waiting for the bus to take me down & around

as a black umbrella, black leather coat &
black old fashioned leather briefcase stops
his full steam aheading (away from lunch?)
& starts full steaming towards me –
not stopping until his full on, full frontal
almost pre-recorded "I apologise" apologies
& would have whether long lunch or no long lunch
but yes, definitely a long lunch.
I question or half-question why
but we both know why: he lost it
where he shouldn't lose it – in the seminar.
Still, I have to be careful. Okay
I'm more than equal to him right now
but we're not really equals, are we?
I mean we are & we aren't, aren't we?
I give as good as I get, I say
but I know he knows I know he lost it.
Saying it's no excuse, he excuses himself
with the flu. Again & then again. At last
he doesn't say he has a tendency to
repeat himself. He just repeats himself.
Well, if I'm a student, I'm a student.
"I'm not sure how I'm going. How _am_ I going?"
The same as he wrote in red, almost word for word.
More clarity, please. He wants more clarity
tripping over three words every sentence.

He has had quite a few glasses, he says
& when I can't help smiling he says
"You noticed". It's the quote of the week.
Now he's on about chance meetings
about the importance of the unimportant –
the anarchic, the arbitrary, the accidental
the roll of the dice, the flip of a coin
the fall of a raindrop off the tip of a pine needle
if not a special providence in the fall of
a sulphur-crested, white cockatoo.

Will he say I'll remember this meeting
longer than Flinders remembered Baudin
longer than Baudin remembered or
I'll remember Flinders?

No, he won't. Not now, not here, anyway
but he will, he probably will.
So I probably won't.

GRAHAM ROWLANDS

LIMBO IS DEAD

Now that His Holiness the Pope
has pronounced the death of Limbo
there's no longer any possibility of
a Medieval monk's quill & inkwell
becoming a secular Too Hard basket;
no longer any possibility of
Limbo making some sort of comeback
as an African Commander-in-Chief
as President Limbo or Limbo Limbo.
Although Hell is still in limbo
& Heaven is still in limbo
& Purgatory is still in limbo
Limbo is no longer in limbo.
Before Limbo was in limbo, though
Limbo was just plain Limbo. Now
Limbo is dead, dead as dead children.

GRAHAM ROWLANDS

THE PLANE TREE

It has taken months of autumn
to dry & curl the plane tree's
green to grey & rust & brown.
When I turn off the light
I swivel in my chair &
turn on the panel of light
to catch a branch of
north-eastern leaves. By
mid-afternoon I'm again
looking up from dark into light
the early blistered leaves
now shadows filtering
the north-western blaze.

I could believe in
this tree's longevity
long after this room, these rooms
are hosed down to dust

long after the earth
has gone around in a
last rendezvous
with the sun.

I could believe in
the light rusting the leaves
the leaves rusting the light

if I were a believer.

GRAHAM ROWLANDS

PORTRAIT

She chooses that chair, then
at the family gathering
opposite the entrance
giving her a first rate view
her feet planted square as Queen Anne legs.

Her eyes are dim with age and her permed hair
is barely able to hold a tinge of brown.
She has that perpetual smile, on lips
pushed firmly to the front by a palisade of teeth
that trap you tightly outside.
Her cardigan drapes over the polished arms
like the too-soft folds of her kindness.

She wears emotion as a tool to prise
the gaps of others' weakness; it flakes easily
like cheap paint, not the real thing
which I saw once, as she bent to kiss
the ghostly lips of her husband near death,
and it shocked me, moved me.

ROS SCHULZ

HUMPTY DUMPTY

forever glueing together
pieces of fractured shell
filling the cracks
and sanding them smooth
so that at first glance
you might think
that I have never fallen
and broken

VERONICA SHANKS

HER HENS PREFER MOZART

Busy bistro,
aromatic coffee wafts:
around one table,
a group of women
chatter in fiftyish camaraderie,
even confide some secrets.
like:
"One of my hens,
the one I call Blade,
once sat on my chest
while I slept on the lounge.
When I woke up,
there she was,
nestled on my heart."

The others look bemused.

"The hens are among my best friends,"
she continues,
"They come inside and squat
in a semi-circle round the piano
while I play."
Downy softness veils her eyes.

Silence weighs on the others.
Hens don't feature in their lives.
they fret about,
cholesterol,
cellulite,
smile lines,
sun damage to their skins,
ageing husbands,
whether to redecorate the lounge.

Of course,
they eat an egg or two each week –
reach for free range
and kid themselves that all is OK.
Their lives are too frenetic
to connect with hens.

ALICE SHORE

TO SIR, WITH LOVE

I? Exiled amongst the Beautiful young under-grads,
who belonged, <u>you</u>, of few,
were all interest: *in* me.

Not long ago on an early Gawler train
I saw you, Sir.
On you, the morning's sunshine a halo.
Moving towards the front
in your fuzzy red jumper and actual tweed.
And I blessed you, Sir,
for teaching a few doomed youth to read:
allowing them to slip Rap's tight lasso.

And I blessed you, Sir,
and ached to say hello:
have some of your goodness touch me.
But I sat at the back, Sir,
with my Magdalene baggage
and a few other, unlikely, reprobates.
And I didn't want to smirch you

You were reading, Sir,
perhaps even poetry: such concentration.
Its balm nourishing you: before your students' need.
Affording me this passive infusion.
Stronger, though, for us,
than a line of coke:
to kick start the day.

A. M. SLADDIN

PRIME APES

The few, last reading apes
gather in the remnant garden.
Mad-dog-hot they cower under the trees' sundial respite:
slivers of shade.

The few, last reading apes
no longer climb trees.
Can barely climb hills,
they hunch again,
re-Simian.
The friendly
amongst the few, last reading apes
brush grass from each other's backs:
mimicking the pick of nits.
While I sit.
A lone
sentry.

A. M. SLADDIN

TWINS

I leave my twin boys three days, or four,
around Christmas: they're fine.
One eats too much, the other not enough:
though there's hardly anything between 'em.
One is quite sooky, but plays hard too get.
The other doesn't care but is cuddly.
I only smack 'em, fairly, soft: when they need it.
And I haven't shaken them.

I drowned the rooster in a bucket, but,
they still wake up all night anyway.
When they grizzle,
too much,
and want my love, attention,
I shut some doors.
To hear their quick-sand demands no more.
To sleep through their demise.

But kittens climb sooner than apes,
and, up in the ceiling
they dance themselves into vigour:
disturbing my sleep.
Awake, out to the loo,
they follow me inside
to a midnight feast
to the warm nest where
we three curl in sleep.

A. M. SLADDIN

FEAST YOUR EYES

My hands in dishwater
I am bathed in pink light
from the sunset.
Vibrant citrus yellow,
mandarin orange
leaking into watermelon, raspberries
and dobs of blueberry ice-cream
garnished by mint-leaf trees.
A feast for my eyes
makes me want to lean
from the window,
and lick the sky.

CAROLYN STIRLING CROSHAW

PORT AUGUSTA ROAD TRIP

car engine hummed
over the bitumen highway
skirting a tumbleweed hitchhiker
as the loudspeaker wind
vacuumed paddocks of their top soil

red dust
eclipsed a strand
of pepper trees
& crimson fleeced lambs
bleat for ewes

COLLEEN SWEENEY

WOMAN IN 4
for Kris

1

accidental baby drops from her womb
she flees,
naked and doped
leaving father and child to Cohen's consolations

2

found her in body shop
speeding to salvation
brothel hooks, money's fast
she learns that not all tricks are magic

3

needles and fucks
hep C for lunch
I watch her slip into the vein of junk
nod her way to the valley of absolution

4

holy white holy death statistic junkie whore
she floated
toxic beauty . . .
could never really find the ground.

JENNY TOUNE

A THOUGHT IS NOT AN INSTINCT

pushing back the edges of depression – it's a quick-sand of insanity and I want to scream out "no!" but the sand fills my mouth and I am drawn down into a deep and genuine paralysis of ennui. a thought is not an instinct.

blind. finding my level like water that creeps up to my nostrils in the night when there's nobody watching. my other senses are heightened but not high enough for me to climb out of here. a thought is not an instinct.

the angry cello of depression strikes a chord in my gut like a cat climbing the curtains of a burning ship while the orchestra keeps on playing, keeps on playing; the angry cello keeps on playing. a thought is not an instinct.

howl. till I'm tearing up photographs and dancing with the moon. crippled kittens and limp spirits join in wanting excess and everything that goes with it so I lite up a cigarette to shut out the rain. a thought is not an instinct.

KERRYN TREDREA

BENT

I like the curves
like the ones on my '94 Celica
(and yes it is red)

like the ones on your girlfriend
and on the rollicking hillside.

(these are not similes
rather incomplete love stories)

I like the curves of the roads
in the hills you like to speed on.

The curves of your wife
and her best friend.

The curves on a bottle of
Napoleon.

The curves of my bed head
and your body around mine.

PETER TSATSOULIS

NO SHOES AND THE DAY WAS FREEZING

She was tiny
staring up at me
eyes wide open, expressionless
strands of filthy nit-ridden hair
hanging down her face
ribbons of snot oozing from her nostrils

A dirty cotton dress, two sizes too big
a shoulder strap hanging over an arm
a once white singlet edged with torn lace
covered a thin chest.
her limbs were emaciated
no shoes and the day was freezing . . .

What thoughts were there
in that four year old mind?
what expectations did she have?
what future would be hers?

Her eyes never wavered
was I a threat?
was I an opportunity?
then she came to me
arms stretched upwards
asking me to lift her.
this wasn't right
no normal child should want
a hug from a stranger

Despite my horror of snot
despite the pervasive smell of shit
despite knowing it was wrong
I lifted her
with mucus smearing my shirt
my shirt sleeve growing wet
from the damp patch on her dress
I laid her head on my shoulder

And for a moment
I loved that tiny child
my feelings overwhelming
my pain physical
my son was her age
I wiped away my tears.

KEN VINCENT

THE PENULTIMATE POET

Not last in line
only second last.
Not quite the pits
simply second worst.
Not the last resort
or an afterthought;
no final spurt
of just desserts;
not heady draughts
but modest tipples.
Not making waves
just spreading ripples.

JULIA WAKEFIELD

PHRASED OUT

I only speak a little . . .
No, I don't understand.
Where can I get a map?
How much do I need to pay?
Excuse me, I'm sorry.
Where's the toilet?

Could you please repeat that?
No, I don't understand.
Do you speak English?
Does anyone speak English?
Excuse me, I'm sorry.
Where's the toilet?

No, I don't want to buy it.
How long will it be delayed?
Excuse me – *that's my seat!*
I'm sorry, no. No. No. No.
Do I need a special permit?
Where's the toilet?

I didn't order this.
It's against my religion / beliefs.
Stop that! You're annoying.
Excuse me, *excuse me!*
I want to contact my embassy . . .
Where's the toilet?

I don't want to stop at the carpet shop.
I need a doctor who speaks English.
I'm sorry, excuse me, *no*,
excuse me, no, I'm sorry.
I didn't know I had to declare it.
I only speak a little.

AMELIA WALKER

CHLORIDE STREET CUT UP

I'd forgotten
the road is a long as
silence
soft as feathers
perched on sharp rock.

All these machines
have left an imprint on my
naked
heart
making me feel like a down town rapper
with flies in my eyes.

I only see
glints and sparkles
spit on the sidewalk
patchworks of
somewhere
everywhere
darkness.

You talk of
deadly times
the world upside down.
Nothing makes me happier.
History
smells like
the dogs next door.
The earth is
heavy with road kill.

We are
our silhouette
a river of air
relentless in its rolling
blank faced
as the sky.
We are our past
our present
our future
with everything / nothing to say

AMELIA WALKER

This poem was written while I was poet-in-residence in Broken Hill.
The cottage I stayed in had a sun room where other poets had written
poems on the wall. I took at least one word from every other poem and
composed this one. The line breaks signify a change of poem.

SHE TOLD HIM HER NAME

and he took it, held it on his tongue
– giddy as vodka
infused with sherbet: everything
good about childhood,
poured into a glass the shape of dying.
She told him her name

and he swallowed it in one go
like the seed of a chocolate watermelon;
recalled the movie *Junior*, wondered
if stomach might double as womb. He wanted
to be consumed by his own consumption, wanted
its vines to dislodge his organs, scream
from eyesnosemouthears. She
told him her name

and it was the only name he'd ever heard,
the only sound – his unspoken first word;
it was falling from the top floor,
never hitting the ground;
it was an unlived memory, a stitched-up promise,
a shattered vase of Mondays, a wound
healed more beautiful than before.
She told him her name

and he tattooed it on his lung;
it was the breath
he couldn't catch,
every word he'd never said.
She told him her name
and he wanted it to be his name too.
She told him her name

as she tiptoed out his front door,
as he stood, half-dressed,
wondering, *was he dreaming?*
She told him her name,
but not her number
and it took the rest of the morning
– two black coffees –
to remember his own.

AMELIA WALKER

ON THIS EARTH

for Deb – a reply

there are two sexes
if you forget about the trannies
men born in women's bodies
women born in men's bodies

on this earth
men love women
women love men
except for the men who love men
and the women who love women
except for the ones who love both
and the ones who love none

on this earth
men work
except for those who don't
women have babies
except for those who can't
or won't

G. M. WALKER

DANNY IN DETENTION

Dad works at Hills but he hasta go to the physio. for his arm. whennie was a kid his bruvva useta twist is arma round. me bruvva & me fight all the time he's 16 I'm 11 but I can bash im up. he's psycho. he calls me pissweak so I bash im. dad belted me. I adta go to bed ungry. me bruvva works at kfc. dozen gimme nuffin. dad's got is own playstation in the lounge. dozen lettuce uzit tho

ROB WALKER

THE DUST OF RHAJASTAN

in the dust of rhajastan there is a bear
with a rope through the hole
       in its nose
             nosing up to the stick of power
             up to hind legs

sad eyes sunk in dusted flyaway hair

the eastern mode of a reedy horn
a listless cobra

three animals all trapped in a loop
       on the rim of extinction

all lashed together in tableau

a snake,
a bear,
a man.

this nexus of pathos
       performing the dance
           tourists no longer
              wish to see

ROB WALKER

SIESTA

Dresses move gently
against white louvre doors
a kind of picket fencing
where ghost women walk.

Circular skirts sway, lift at the hem
kaleidoscope glazed patterns, blue-grey
with white, bright blue-leafed stems
against another's green.

In the glue heat outside
the sky is tin.
Only a stroll away
unfenced jungle waits

where snakes still slide
beneath the screeching monkeys.
Then Sunday splits with thunder
the sudden drum and riff of rain.

JOSIE WALSH

YOU STAYED

Your tiny fingers
Twitch upon my breast
Your life, my life
Your life, my breast
My life, your breath

Each starfish hand
Spread, now clenched
Now lifted, stretched
Above your head
I hear you sigh
I sigh

Tiny body
Tiny boy
You stayed.

SARAH WAUCHOPE

For further information about
Friendly Street publications and activities please visit
our website: friendlystreetpoets.org.au
email: poetry@friendlystreetpoets.org.au
postal: PO Box 3697 Norwood SA 5067